Free of Me

free of Me

Why Life Is Better When It's
NOT ABOUT YOU

SHARON HODDE MILLER

BakerBooks
a division of Baker Publishing Group
Grand Rapids, Michigan

© 2019 by Sharon Hodde Miller

Published by Baker Books
a division of Baker Publishing Group
PO Box 6287, Grand Rapids, MI 49516-6287
www.bakerbooks.com

Printed in the United States of America

ISBN 978-0-8010-7815-6

Portions of this text have been taken from *Free of Me*, published by Baker Books, 2017.

Author is represented by The Christopher Ferebee Agency, www. christopherferebee.com.

19 20 21 22 23 24 25   7 6 5 4 3 2 1

Contents

Introduction

"L ive your best life."

Oprah may have popularized the sentiment a decade ago, but now it's everywhere. Messages urging us to be our best *us* abound on every inspirational corner, from the Hallmark aisle to our Instagram feeds.

We live in a culture that's simply all about *self*, becoming the best "me" I can be. There is, of course, much value in personal growth. But what the culture *doesn't* focus on is the ultimate pursuit: becoming like Jesus.

This me-centered message can permeate every area of our lives—our friendships, families, self-image, even faith—and it has the opposite effect it's meant to: it negatively impacts each part of our lives. The self-focused life robs our joy, shrinks our souls, and is the reason we never quite break free of insecurity.

I want to invite you to take part in a five-part video series and this corresponding workbook based on my book *Free of Me*. Through this series, we'll explore a bigger, Jesus-centered vision—one that restores our freedom and inspires us to live for more. Let's enter into this gloriously freeing revelation that life isn't about me.

Lord, may this study reveal the things that cause self-focus in our lives, and equip us to set our eyes on you and others instead of on ourselves. May it help us seek to discover something bigger than "project me" and to experience freedom from the burden of self-focus and joy in the light of your higher purpose. Amen.

Session 1

Three Myths of Self-Focus

Are you looking for accolades? Are you looking for applause? Are you looking for approval? Are you looking for acceptance? Because those things will kill you. The Devil will make sure you get all of that. Especially early, and especially young, so that you then collapse when you're unapplauded, when you're unapproved, when you're unaccepted, and when you're unwanted.

Christine Caine

This is a story about a woman who didn't realize she had made her life all about her.

She was a woman so focused on her self-image that her relationships with God and others and her attitude toward herself suffered. She maintained perfect social media platforms, volunteered for every church event, and did everything she could to be the "perfect Christian woman." Over time, she became exhausted with trying to maintain the perfect image.

That woman was me. I thought my focus was on God. I was wrong.

If someone were to ask you, "Is your focus on God?" you'd want to answer, "Yes!" right? After all, you probably are deeply faithful and have an active prayer life—interceding for yourself and your family but also, heartily, for your friends and the people in your circle. And you love God's Word. You engage in a community of faith. You long to glorify Jesus. It's all true, no doubt, but what happens when you see a mirror? Do you immediately look at your own reflection or beyond it?

Honestly, we are all more focused on ourselves than we might think. Our self-preoccupation affects everything—our relationships, our jobs, our self-image. We tend to make everything about us, but the reality is that following Christ is *not* about us.

In this first session, let's open our hearts to the truth that we are more self-focused than we think, and certainly more than we want to be. I'll introduce what I call the "mirror reflex"—our tendency to look at ourselves in a reflective surface no matter where we are, losing sight of our true purpose. And in this session, we'll start the journey of what pastor Tim Keller calls "self-forgetfulness." We'll start the journey of being *free of me*.

Before watching video 1, read the introduction and chapters 1, 2, and 14 in *Free of Me*.

1. Do you relate to Adrian's story? If so, has being a "good Christian" become a "terrible master" in your life?

_____

_____

_____

_____

_____

_____

_____

_____

_____

_____

_____

_____

_____

_____

_____

_____

_____

_____

_____

_____

2. Does the idea of the mirror reflex ring true to you? How so? How have you seen it manifest in your own life?

_____

_____

_____

_____

_____

_____

_____

_____

_____

_____

_____

_____

_____

_____

_____

_____

_____

_____

3. *For many of us, the problem is not that we think poorly about our-selves. The problem is that we can't stop thinking about ourselves.* If the root of insecurity is low self-esteem and self-preoccupation, how do you manage insecurity and its causes? To what or whom do you turn, and what messages do you embrace?

_____

_____

_____

_____

_____

_____

How can you replace those messages that lead to insecurity with ones of self-forgetfulness?

_____

_____

_____

_____

_____

_____

_____

13

4. Read and pray over Psalm 139:23–24. How does the Holy Spirit speak to you through this passage? What's the difference between being a "good Christian" and living in the way everlasting?

_____

_____

_____

_____

_____

_____

_____

_____

_____

_____

_____

_____

_____

_____

_____

_____

5. Read and pray over Hebrews 12:1–2. In light of the mirror reflex, and knowing about the ancient story of Narcissus, how do you fix your eyes on Jesus?

_____

_____

_____

_____

_____

_____

_____

_____

_____

_____

_____

_____

_____

_____

_____

_____

6. *[Jesus] knew better than anyone that healing is a sign of the king-dom of God, not a lesser priority or a thing to be rushed. Jesus also understood that we cannot "run the race marked out for us" (Heb. 12:1) if we are too wounded even to stand.* As you take stock of your self-focus and its unfortunate by-product, insecurity, what healing do you see needs to be done so you can run the race set out for you by Christ?

_____

_____

_____

_____

_____

_____

_____

_____

_____

_____

_____

_____

_____

_____

_____

_____

_____

7. Understanding the difference between self-focus and confidence is sometimes difficult. Why do we so easily confuse them? How can we tell the difference?

_____

_____

_____

_____

_____

_____

_____

_____

_____

_____

_____

_____

_____

_____

_____

8. *The problem is not the body but the* flesh, *the human power that opposes dependence on God.* What is the difference between forgetting yourself and neglecting yourself? How do you do one but not the other?

_____

_____

_____

_____

_____

_____

_____

_____

_____

_____

_____

_____

_____

_____

Session 2

When You Make God about You

> You can safely assume you've created God in your own image when it turns out that God hates all the same people as you do.
>
> Anne Lamott

We can often start to think that God exists for us. It's pretty easy to do, because sometimes, despite our best efforts, we can confuse our own voice with God's. In a conflict, for instance, it's easy for our prayers for wisdom to morph into a self-righteous rant about how the other person was wrong. And thus, it can become easy to assume that God agrees with us.

In so many instances, we can make God "in our own image." We can start to believe that God's very purpose is to help, serve, or exalt us. We believe incorrect things about his character and focus our relationship with him on ourselves and what he gives us.

And although it's an easy trap to fall into, believing God looks and thinks like us, we know, of course, that he doesn't. We know intellectually that God's purpose isn't to reflect *us*. We have the most beautiful, glorious identity in Christ, but let us not confuse things. Our identity is in Christ, but Christ's identity is not in us. The danger in reversing these roles is that we create a false god.

As beings made in *God's* image, and created to worship, let us lift our praise to him.

In this session, I want us to consider what truly reflecting our Creator can look like. Before watching video 2, read chapters 3 and 10 in *Free of Me*.

1. Kaley explained in this video that she had a transactional relationship with God—that God owed her blessings in return for "good behavior." Do you find that to be true in areas of your own life?

_____

_____

_____

_____

_____

_____

_____

_____

_____

_____

_____

_____

_____

_____

_____

2. There are four key false gods we tend to make God into. The self-help god, the self-serving god, the self-exalting god, and the self-image god. Have you worshiped any of these false gods? If so, which ones?

_____

_____

_____

_____

_____

_____

Begin to consider Why? What drew you to the place where you made God in your own image?

_____

_____

_____

_____

_____

_____

_____

_____

3. *When we make God about us, we miss something essential about him and ourselves. The "special sauce" of the gospel is not that it makes us feel good but that it calls us into something bigger than ourselves.* What is that bigger thing? That bigger vision? Why is it so crucial that we deny these false gods and seek that bigger thing? And what are the potential consequences of nurturing them?

_____

_____

_____

_____

_____

_____

_____

_____

_____

_____

_____

_____

_____

_____

4. *When our train of thought goes off the rails, we have to intervene. We have to stop the train.* What trains of thought that distract you from God's purpose for you are most difficult for you to stop?

_____

_____

_____

_____

_____

Many of us have read Luke 10:27 many times. But read it again, and let it sink in. What makes this verse so key in derailing the locomotive of self-focus?

_____

_____

_____

_____

_____

_____

_____

_____

_____

_____

5. Read and pray over Philippians 1:15–18. How does Paul's confidence speak to you? Do you feel the same sense of confidence? Why or why not?

_____

_____

_____

_____

_____

_____

_____

_____

_____

_____

_____

_____

_____

_____

_____

_____

6. *What I didn't realize until recently is that worship isn't simply our purpose. It isn't just a good thing to do or a godly thing to do. It's also our help. Worship awakens us, heals us, and rescues us.* Worshiping God rescues us from ourselves. It turns our eyes from our pursuits, our lack of perspective, our insecurities and fears and sometimes-skewed priorities and reminds us, as the old saying goes, that God is God and I am not. How do you express worship in your life? Are there places in your life where you've found a worshipful rhythm? And are there places you've seemed to neglect or even actively pushed away a worshipful posture? How can the truly worshipful experiences in your life inform the ones that are lacking?

7. Read my (totally not exhaustive!) list of God's attributes on page 136. This list has helped me time and time again to stop my self-focus train, to remind me that we were *created* for praise. Are there particular attributes on this list that speak to you, that reach the place where you've avoided a posture of praise?

_____

_____

_____

_____

_____

_____

_____

_____

_____

_____

_____

_____

_____

_____

_____

Session 3

When You Make Family about You

Loving someone liberates the lover as well as the beloved.

Maya Angelou

Have you ever seen something your child or spouse or friend did and thought, *Yikes, that's embarrassing.* If you haven't, can you please write a book describing in detail how you avoided it? I'm kidding, of course, because I honestly don't know *anyone* who hasn't at one point felt embarrassed by someone they love. Whether your husband has told the same story at parties over and over again or your child performed less than epically on the soccer field, there are moments when we feel a tug of shame about our loved ones.

If we do manage to notice the Holy Spirit waving the flag, saying "Hello! Who do you think *you* are?" even still we may not realize *why* we're embarrassed in the first place. The truth is we expect our loved ones to represent us. It's a kind of self-focus that is sneaky at best and detrimental to our relationships with people and God at worst.

When we assume our relationships are meant just for us, we can hurt the people who matter most to us. But God's purpose for our relationships is not for them to represent some curated, ideal version of ourselves but rather to provide a uniquely beautiful and precious space for us to love him and love others.

In this session, I want us to unpack what it means to seek God and others via our family relationships and friendships. Let's aim to reframe our relationships to be about how God's love and truth can shine within them.

Before watching video 3, read chapters 4, 7, and 11 in *Free of Me*.

1. *Image management . . . it's exactly how it sounds: when you "manage" how people see you. It takes an endless number of forms, like the need to appear attractive, happy, successful, organized, or smart, and just like the mirror reflex, it treats everything in your life as a reflection on you.* In what areas of your life are you most prone to image management?

2. Like Melanie from the video, do you ever find yourself hiding in order to maintain your image?

_____

_____

_____

_____

_____

_____

_____

_____

_____

_____

_____

_____

_____

_____

_____

_____

3. It's *so* easy to think that our family's purpose is about us. We face pressures from all sides, but mostly from ourselves, to be the family we think we should be, to look the way we think we should, to engage with one another in the way we think seems most impressive. Even our attempts to glorify God via our families can sometimes become pressure points, places where we feel the need to look or act the part. Have you felt the pressure to act the part, and how has it affected your relationships?

_____

_____

_____

Have you felt the pressure put on *you* to be a certain way for someone else? How did it affect you?

_____

_____

What strategies can help you worry less about your image and more about loving your family members as God loves them? What does that love look like?

_____

_____

_____

_____

33

4. The martyr complex can make its way into the way we manage our
   families as well. It seems counterintuitive, but sometimes we neglect
   ourselves to make our families look perfect. Has this been a temptation for you? In what ways have you neglected yourself in order
   to appear perfect? What steps can you take to move beyond that
   temptation?

_____

_____

_____

_____

_____

_____

_____

_____

_____

_____

_____

_____

_____

5. As with our families, we can assume our friendships are about us too. Whether we experience a moment of rejection, a snub, or loneliness because we aren't part of a fulfilling Christian community, we can forget that friendships are about helping us seek and show God's love rather than taming our insecurities. Has rejection or loneliness shaped your self-image, and if so, how? How might God use those wounds to make you a true friend?

_____

_____

_____

_____

_____

_____

_____

_____

_____

_____

_____

_____

_____

6. *Love God. Love others. According to Romans 13:9, the whole law can be "summed up" in those four words, and for most of my life I have tried to live by them. But here's what I always got wrong: for too long, I viewed these commands as "good Christian behavior." . . . What I'm discovering, however, is that God's desire has always been much bigger and better than being good. . . . God asks us to love others because it glorifies him and it heals something deep inside of us. . . . There is a second way to joy, which is loving people.* John 15:13 says, "Greater love has no one than this: to lay down one's life for one's friends." God's vision for family and friendships is for us to love God and love others. But what does it mean to lay down our lives for them? Who might God be calling you to love better? Why does that person come to mind, and what steps can you take to show that love?

_____

_____

_____

_____

_____

_____

_____

_____

_____

_____

7. There's a big difference between shame and humility. Shame makes everything a referendum on our identity and worth, but Jesus's sacrifice was a direct affront to shame. Humility is about possessing an identity firmly rooted in Christ. And humility—not shame—is one of the ways we can conquer image management. But being humble is easier said than done. How can Jesus's own humble sacrifice for us influence the way you learn to humble yourself without falling prey to shame?

_____

_____

_____

_____

_____

_____

_____

_____

_____

_____

_____

_____

_____

_____

Session 4

When You Make
Appearance and
Possessions about You

Vanity costs money, labor, horses, men, women, health, and peace,
and is still nothing at last.

Ralph Waldo Emerson

Not a single one of us is immune to the constant influx of messages the world sends us about appearance. The world tells us we will be happy if we fit into this pair of jeans or if our lawn looks like that. The pretty happy message never stops, not when it comes to our physical appearance, not when it comes to our possessions, not when it comes to our image in general.

What's particularly alarming about these messages is the clear intent: they want to remind us that we are weak and falling short, and they want us to endlessly strive to hide those feelings of inadequacy. And in fact, they're drawing on original human behavior. After all, Adam and Eve tried to hide their sin by hiding their bodies. In the same way, we try to hide our fears about growing older with hair dye and diet plans.

While our preoccupation with having the perfect life is understandable, left unchecked and uncorrected it can wreak havoc on our souls. Instead of calling us to have the perfect life, God calls us to be openhearted, honest, and generous and to join in Christ's suffering.

In this session, I'd like us to counter the world's standards of appearance and possessions with God's call for us to be like Jesus, a much greater call indeed. Before watching video 4, read chapters 5, 6, and 13 in *Free of Me*.

1. Do you relate to Tiffany's story? If so, do you share her concerns that she had taken her interest in her appearance too far?

_____

_____

_____

_____

_____

_____

_____

_____

_____

_____

_____

_____

_____

_____

_____

_____

_____

_____

2. First Timothy 6:17 says, "Command those who are rich in this present world not to be arrogant nor to put their hope in wealth, which is so uncertain, but to put their hope in God, who richly provides us with everything for our enjoyment." In what things, besides God, are you most tempted to put your hope? What does it mean to put your hope in God, and how can you pivot your focus?

3. *The challenge, then, is not to forget our appearances or to downplay them, but to remember what they are for. And what they are not for. Too often, appearance becomes a relational barrier, when God intended it as a bridge.* Read and pray over Philippians 2:5–8. What does this passage say about your physical appearance and its purpose in light of how Jesus saw himself?

_____

_____

_____

_____

_____

_____

_____

_____

_____

_____

_____

_____

_____

_____

_____

_____

4. Have you ever felt competitive with someone else? Is there someone you're jealous of or someone with whom you secretly compete? How does that competition cause you to act? To feel?

_____

_____

_____

_____

_____

_____

_____

How can the pursuit of modesty—not in terms of how clothing covers us but in terms of how much we flaunt ourselves—help you reject the culture of competition?

_____

_____

_____

_____

_____

_____

_____

_____

5. *The root word of "vanity," vanus, means "empty," which is the perfect word picture for both vanity and greed.* How do vanity and greed keep us from being generous? And what does it mean to choose "compassion over comparison?"

_____

_____

_____

_____

_____

How can choosing compassion over comparison help shift your focus away from competition with friends and neighbors?

_____

_____

_____

_____

_____

_____

_____

_____

6. Jesus says in John 12:24, "Unless a kernel of wheat falls to the ground and dies, it remains only a single seed. But if it dies, it produces many seeds." This verse says that the way to new life is through death, a theme and a truth repeated over and over again in Scripture. How does sharing in Christ's suffering help you shift your focus away from trying to have a perfect life?

_____

_____

_____

_____

_____

_____

_____

_____

_____

_____

_____

_____

_____

_____

_____

_____

7. *That is the strange, surprising, upside-down good news of Jesus Christ. Whenever you feel like a failure or a hack, whenever you worry that you're not a good parent or spouse, whenever you fear you're not enough or that you can't keep up with it all, there is a sense in which God responds, "Yes, that's true." And this is, amazingly, good news.* Why is this good news? How can it help you "*be better* instead of *feeling* better?"

Session 5

When You Make Calling about You

Work is . . . the full expression of the worker's faculties, the thing in which he finds spiritual, mental, and bodily satisfaction, and the medium in which he offers himself to God.

Dorothy Sayers

Most of us have a vision for what we want for our lives. Whether it's specific (a career path or life trajectory) or vague (a certain hope we have for our future), we all tend to make plans for ourselves. And it's easy to get so caught up in those plans that we take all the steps we believe we need to take in order to reach our goals. Often, our prayers in light of our calling can center around how to achieve the things we hope for, while we forget to listen for the Holy Spirit's guidance as to whether these are the things God wants for us in the first place. We've made our entire calling about us without even realizing it.

We make our calling about us by assuming we know exactly what God wants for us. And we make our church about us by wanting it to be exactly

49

what we want it to be, all the time. I didn't realize this at first, but self-focus and consumerism had permeated my thinking about both elements in my life. Perhaps they have done the same in your life as well.

God gives us a calling and places us in a body of believers for both our good *and* the good of others. When we make our calling about us, we miss out on that purpose.

In this session, we'll talk about God's purpose for our calling and how we can separate our consumerism from our participation with God and our communities. Before watching video 5, read chapters 8, 9, and 12 in *Free of Me*.

1. Do you know what your calling is? How so, and what is it? If you've never thought about it, is there something that immediately comes to mind? Consider what that might be and why the Lord may have placed it on your heart.

———————————————————————————

———————————————————————————

———————————————————————————

———————————————————————————

———————————————————————————

———————————————————————————

———————————————————————————

———————————————————————————

———————————————————————————

———————————————————————————

———————————————————————————

———————————————————————————

———————————————————————————

———————————————————————————

———————————————————————————

———————————————————————————

2. *Your successes only provide you with a fleeting joy. If your calling is a personal measuring stick, then your self-esteem will depend on the day. Did you make the deal? Did you get the promotion? . . . Each one of these successes or failures can influence your contentment and your self-worth, which is the power and the danger of making your calling about you.* Have you experienced dissatisfaction with your calling? In what ways?

_____

_____

_____

_____

_____

_____

_____

_____

_____

_____

_____

_____

_____

3. Like Kara, have you ever felt your calling shift or even fall out from beneath your feet? How did you respond?

_____

_____

_____

_____

_____

_____

_____

_____

_____

_____

_____

_____

_____

_____

_____

_____

_____

_____

_____

4. Read and consider Philippians 4:11–12. How is being content in all things related to your calling in life? Perhaps contentment is a simple way of expressing the truly incredible experience of being within God's will. God's calling is compelling and fulfilling, and one of the consequences of making our calling about us is disobedience. Why? How can these verses bring you back to obeying God's plan for you versus your own?

_____

_____

_____

_____

_____

_____

_____

_____

_____

_____

_____

_____

_____

_____

5. As we begin to close out this series, there is one final place where our self-focus can distract us from God, and shockingly, it's in the church. As I mentioned in the book, consumerism is a hallmark of modern society. Are there any parts of your church that frustrate you because they're not how you would do them? What might God be teaching you through those things?

_____

_____

_____

_____

_____

_____

_____

_____

_____

_____

_____

_____

_____

_____

_____

_____

6. Read Isaiah 49:6. To me, this verse encapsulates the entire idea behind *Free of Me*. God is telling the Israelites that their vision for what God can do through them is "too small a thing." God wants to save not just the tribes of Jacob but *the whole world*. We know that's the ultimate vision for us Christians too—to bring God's light to the whole world. What an incredible truth, a huge responsibility. Knowing now all the ways self-focus can distract us from this vision, what steps can you take to shift your view and see beyond your own reflection?

_____

_____

_____

_____

_____

_____

_____

_____

_____

_____

_____

_____

_____

7. In this series, what has stood out to you as the most relevant lesson for your own life? What ideas will you take with you?

_____

_____

_____

_____

_____

_____

_____

_____

_____

_____

_____

_____

_____

_____

_____

_____

_____

_____

_____

Final Prayer

Lord, thank you so much for the endless grace you show me every minute of every day. I am overwhelmed by your love, and it humbles me. I know that my life is for you, but sometimes I stray from that knowledge. Thank you for reminding me that your vision is the one that's fulfilling and compelling and that an abundant life and an obedient one are the same. I commit all the parts of my life to your will. Amen.

Sharon Hodde Miller is a writer, speaker, pastor's wife, and mom of two. Sharon is passionate about equipping women with the truths of God, and over the years she has written for numerous sites and publications, including *Her.meneutics*, Propel, She Reads Truth, *Christianity Today* magazine, (in)courage, *Relevant*, The Gospel Project, and Gifted for Leadership, in addition to her personal blog, *SheWorships.com*. Sharon earned her master of divinity at Duke Divinity School and her PhD at Trinity Evangelical Divinity School, where she researched women and calling. Sharon and her family live in North Carolina, where she loves serving the women at her church and in her community.

Turn Your Focus from

Self to Savior

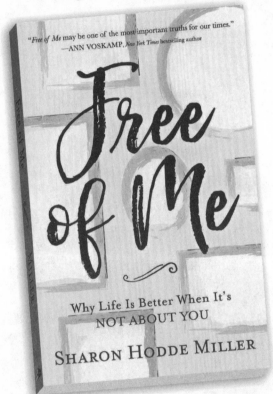

> "In a culture captivated by self, this book is a must-read."
>
> —CHRISTINE CAINE, founder of A21 and Propel Women

Connect with
Sharon!

To learn more about Sharon's
writing and speaking, visit

SheWorships.com

 SharonHoddeMiller   SHoddeMiller   SharonHMiller